Brandywine Hundred Library
1300 Foulk Rd.
Wilmington, DE 19803

W9-BAG-015

Baby Animals

LIONS

Kate Petty

Stargazer Books

Newborn lion cubs

All the lionesses in a family produce their cubs at about the same time. After 16 weeks of pregnancy, a mother lion settles down somewhere quiet to give birth. She may have just one cub, or as many as five.

The mother licks the newborn cubs clean. Each tiny cub weighs 2-4 lbs and is nearly 24 inches long—about the same size as a large domestic cat.

The cubs have their first wash.

This lioness will have her babies soon. ▶

The first few weeks

The lion cubs are totally helpless at first. Like most babies, they spend the majority of their time asleep. Their eyes stay closed until they are about ten days old.

For the first three months, the cubs drink milk greedily from their mother—they have a lot of growing to do. Their mother leaves them in a safe hiding place when she goes hunting.

The cubs are blind and completely dependent on their mother.

Milk is the only food these two-week-old cubs need. ▶

Getting about

While the cubs are small, the mother carries them about in her mouth. She grips them by the loose skin of their neck so she won't hurt them.

The cubs soon learn to stagger about. After six weeks, they are quite steady on their feet. Their mother still watches them carefully and carries them back if they stray too far.

A perfectly comfortable way for a cub to travel

The cub is well camouflaged by its spotted coat. ▶

New members

When the cubs are about five weeks old, the lioness takes them to join her family. A family of lions is called a pride. Lions are the only big cats to live in a group like this. They hunt, play, and rest together.

The male lions defend the pride. They leave the care of the cubs to the lionesses but they are very tolerant and protective of their own babies.

The cubs take their place in the family.

A cub is in no danger from its own father. ▶

Family relationships

The lionesses in a pride are all related. The cubs grow up with their cousins, in the care of their mother, aunts, great-aunts, and grandmother.

The cubs drink milk from their mother but they will also feed from other lionesses occasionally. The male lions of the pride are the fathers of the cubs. They watch over the cubs while the lionesses are hunting.

A family group

Female lions are patient mothers. ▶

Mealtime

Animals that live in groups must learn to wait their turn. Although the female lions do the hunting, the male lions have the first share of the food!

When the males have had enough to eat, the female lions and the cubs take their turn. This may seem unfair, but it ensures that the strongest members of the group survive.

Time for the lioness and her cubs to eat!

Father and son drink together. ▶

Playtime

Like kittens, lion cubs spend a lot of time playing. The cubs that become friends while playing together are likely to work well as a hunting team when they are older.

Adult lions are extremely fierce animals, but they are patient and playful with their mischievous cubs. Mother lions may swish their tails and cuff their cubs if they are naughty.

Cubs play fighting

Only a cub would dare to bite a lioness's tail! ▶

Learning

The cubs learn and practice some very important skills as they play. One day, they will have to hunt and kill prey for themselves.

As they creep up on each other, the cubs learn how to stalk their prey. They practice how to catch an animal on the move by pouncing. They also learn by watching and copying their mother as she hunts.

The cub will not be able to catch small animals until he is about nine months old.

Two grubby cubs play fighting ▶

Bedtime

Lions spend a lot of their time lying in the sun or
resting in the shade of a tree. Lions don't have many
enemies in the wild, so they can sleep peacefully.

Sometimes, the whole pride lies down together after
a big meal. The lions are barely visible when they
lie still because the color of their fur blends in with
their surroundings.

Lions resting

A young cub takes a nap. ▶

Older cubs

The cubs continue to grow and learn until they are about two years old. By this time, they are strong enough to look after themselves. Their mother is probably busy with new cubs.

At age three or four, the young lions are able to have babies of their own. The females stay with the pride. The young males leave and live on their own for several years. Eventually, they will take over prides of their own.

Young males leave the pride.

This four-year-old lion isn't yet strong enough to take over a pride. ▶

Lion facts

Lions are members of the cat family. They live in Africa.
At about three months old, the cubs begin to lose their
baby spots and their eyes turn from blue-gray to amber.

A young lion's tail tufts start to grow after five months,
and the male's mane after six months. At about three
years old, the young males are old enough to
leave the pride.

Index

© Aladdin Books Ltd 2005

New edition published in the United States in 2005 by:
Stargazer Books
c/o The Creative Company
123 South Broad Street
P.O. Box 227
Mankato, Minnesota 56002

Designer: Pete Bennett – PBD
Editor: Rebecca Pash
Illustrator: George Thompson
Picture Research: Cee Weston-Baker

Printed in UAE

All rights reserved

Photographic credits:
Cover: PBD; page 3: Ardea; pages 5, 7, 11, 13, 19, and 21: Jonathan Scott / Planet Earth; page 9: Richard Mathews / Planet Earth; page 15: Gunter Ziesler / Bruce Coleman; page 17: G.D. Plage / Bruce Coleman.

Library of Congress Cataloging-in-Publication Data

Petty, Kate.
   Lions / Kate Petty.
   p. cm -- (Baby animals)
   ISBN 1-932799-43-5
   1. Lions--Infancy--Juvenile literature. I. Title.

QL737.C23.P428 2004
599.757'139--dc22

2004040180